Christoph Rothermel

Your Raspberry Pi Smart Home

Setting up your Smart Home with Home
Assistant
- Affordable and Manufacturer Independent

1st Edition

Your Raspberry Pi Smart Home

Your Raspberry Pi Smart Home - Setting up your Smart Home with Home Assistant - Affordable and Manufacturer Independent

The information, procedures, and illustrations in this book have been carefully compiled and tested. However, there is a possibility of errors. Therefore, the information in this book is non-binding and without any warranty. The author assumes no legal responsibility or liability for any damages that may result from the use of this information or parts thereof.

The author cannot guarantee that the described procedures are free from third-party rights. The use of product names, trademarks, and other designations in this book does not imply that they can be considered free from trademark or copyright laws and may be used by anyone.

This work is protected by copyright. All rights, including translation, reprinting, and reproduction of the book or parts thereof, are reserved. Without the written permission of the author, no part of this work may be reproduced or distributed in any form (photocopy, microfilm, or any other method), even for educational purposes, or processed, duplicated, or disseminated using electronic systems.

Printer: Amazon Media EU S.à r.l., 5 Rue Plaetis, L-2338, Luxembourg
Author: Christoph Rothermel, Seydlitzstraße 2/1, 89077 Ulm, Germany; info@rothech.com

ISBN-13: 979-8-8649-5830-8, Independently Published

Preface

Dear readers,

I am delighted to present to you this book about Raspberry Pi Smart Homes. Smart home technologies offer us fascinating opportunities to make our homes smarter and more comfortable. As an enthusiastic tech enthusiast, I have spent a lot of time with Raspberry Pi and Home Assistant, learning a great deal in the process. With this book, I aim to share my knowledge and experiences to make it easier for you to dive into the world of Raspberry Pi Smart Homes.

This book provides a comprehensive guide to setting up and controlling a Raspberry Pi Smart Home. We will delve into the fundamentals of smart home technologies, explore a recommended hardware configuration, and set up Home Assistant step by step. Additionally, you'll find tips on integrating Z-Wave and Zigbee devices, using Alexa and Sonos for voice control and output, as well as setting up push notifications.

Whether you are a beginner or an advanced user, this book is tailored for you. I hope it inspires you and assists you in realizing your own Raspberry Pi Smart Home project.

Enjoy reading, and best of luck with your smart home endeavor!

Yours sincerely,

Christoph

P.S.: Do you have feedback on this book? You are more than welcome to send it to me via email: info@rothech.com

Table of Contents

1 Introduction

Welcome to the exciting world of Raspberry Pi Smart Homes! In this chapter, we will introduce the fundamentals and advantages of a Raspberry Pi Smart Home. Additionally, we will provide an overview of the technologies used and present the structure of the chapters.

1.1 What is a Raspberry Pi Smart Home?

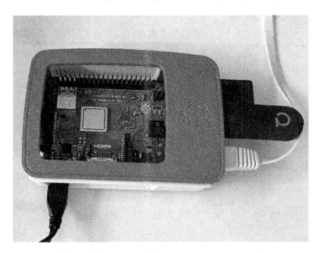

Figure 1 Raspberry Pi Smart Home Hub

You might be wondering what exactly a Raspberry Pi Smart Home is and what benefits it offers. Well, a Raspberry Pi Smart Home is essentially an intelligent home controlled using the small yet powerful Raspberry Pi computer. With this setup, you can automate and control various aspects of your home, ranging from lighting and security to climate control.

The benefits of a Raspberry Pi Smart Home are diverse. Firstly, it enables you to have convenient and centralized control over your entire home automation. You can manage devices and systems through a single user interface and create automated routines that make your home more efficient and comfortable.

Secondly, a Raspberry Pi Smart Home provides you with flexibility and adaptability. Since the Raspberry Pi is based on an open-source platform, you have access to a wide range of software and extension options. You can customize and expand the system to meet your individual needs, adding new features and integrations.

Thirdly, a Raspberry Pi Smart Home allows you to save on energy and operational costs. By automating lighting, heating, ventilation, and other electrical devices, you can optimize energy consumption and, consequently, save money.

Finally, a Raspberry Pi Smart Home also offers a high level of security. You can integrate surveillance cameras, alarm systems, and access control systems to protect your home and detect potential threats.

In summary, a Raspberry Pi Smart Home empowers you to make your home intelligent, enhance comfort and efficiency, save costs, and ensure security.

1.2 Overview of Used Technologies

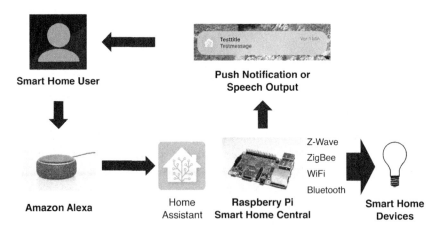

Figure 2 Overview of Technologies

Let's take a brief look at the exciting technologies we will be using for our Raspberry Pi Smart Home. With these tools and devices, you can make your home smart and control it according to your preferences.

Raspberry Pi: The Raspberry Pi will be the core of our Smart Home. With its small size and powerful processing capabilities, it allows us to perform a wide range of tasks and automations.

Home Assistant: Serving as the central technology, Home Assistant enables us to seamlessly link all our smart devices and services. It allows us to create complex automations and manage our Smart Home effortlessly.

Z-Wave and Zigbee: With Z-Wave and Zigbee, we can establish wireless communication with our smart devices. Z-Wave is ideal for controlling lights and blinds, while Zigbee is excellent for integrating sensors such as window and door sensors, as well as temperature sensors.

Amazon Alexa: To control our devices through voice commands, we rely on Amazon Alexa. You can give commands and effortlessly control your Smart Home devices by simply speaking to Alexa.

Sonos: We use Sonos for voice output. This allows you to play your Smart Home systems and notifications in a simple and entertaining manner.

These are just some of the exciting technologies we will be utilizing in our Raspberry Pi Smart Home. In this book, we will delve deeper into them and learn how to successfully integrate them into our project.

1.3 Chapter Structure

The chapters in this book follow a consistent structure to provide you with a clear and practical guide. Each chapter begins with an explanation of the relevant topics, followed by a detailed step-by-step guide for implementation. Finally, each chapter includes a summary of the key points and a list of common errors and potential solutions. This format ensures that you receive both a comprehensive overview and specific solutions for potential challenges.

2 Recommended Hardware Configuration and Cost Calculation

In this chapter, we will introduce the components recommended for your Smart Home. This includes both the Smart Home hub and the components for the Smart Home itself. Additionally, we will explain the hardware setup, including the Raspberry Pi setup and the Smart Home equipment for your apartment or house.

2.1 Recommended Components for Your Smart Home Hub

"The Smart Home hub is the heart of your connected home, connecting and coordinating all smart devices and systems, allowing for centralized control and automation."

Below, we will present the recommended components for your Smart Home hub, including the estimated costs. These components include:

1. The Raspberry Pi 3 or 4 as the core,
2. Power supply,
3. A micro SD card and an SD card reader,
4. An Ethernet cable,
5. A Z-Wave and Zigbee USB stick for Smart Home communication,
6. Optional: a Raspberry Pi case.

These components form the foundation of an effective Smart Home hub.

2.1.1 Raspberry Pi 3 or 4

Figure 3 Raspberry Pi Model 3 B+

The Raspberry Pi is a versatile mini-computer that can be used as the central unit for your Smart Home. You can choose between the Raspberry Pi 3 or 4, depending on your individual requirements and budget. Both models offer powerful features and enable seamless integration of various Smart Home components. The Raspberry Pi serves as the brain of your Smart Home system and serves as the basis for further configurations and automations.

Estimated costs (as of October 2023, source: amazon.com):

- The Raspberry Pi 4 Model B 4GB is currently priced at approximately $66.
- The Raspberry Pi 3 Model B is currently priced at approximately $52.

2.1.2   Power Supply for the Raspberry Pi

Figure 4 Power Supply

Reliable power supply for the Raspberry Pi is crucial to ensure smooth operation. Here are some important aspects to consider regarding power supply:

- **Power Adapter**: Choose a high-quality power adapter with sufficient power output that matches the requirements of your Raspberry Pi model.
- **Power Cable**: Use a suitable USB power cable to connect the Raspberry Pi to the power adapter. Ensure it is of good quality and an adequate length.

Estimated costs (as of October 2023, source: amazon.com):

- The official Raspberry Pi 4 power supply is priced at approximately $15.
- The official Raspberry Pi 3 power supply is priced at approximately $20.

2.1.3 Micro SD Card and SD Card Reader

Figure 5 SD Card

To operate the Raspberry Pi, we need a micro SD card for the operating system and the data of your Smart Home hub. An SD card reader is required for the installation of the operating system.

When researching your purchase, consider the following information:

1. **Micro SD Cards:**

- **Storage Capacity:** Minimum 16 GB. Optimal: 64 GB.

- **Speed Class**: As fast as possible, e.g., Class 10 or UHS-I.

2. **SD Card Reader:**

- **Compatibility:** Ensure that the SD card reader is compatible with the SD cards you intend to use.

- **USB Port:** Choose an SD card reader with a USB port for easy connection to your computer.

A high-quality micro SD card and a reliable SD card reader are crucial for the smooth operation of your Raspberry Pi Smart Home. Be sure to select compatible and high-quality components to ensure optimal performance and storage space for your Smart Home project.

Estimated costs (as of October 2023, source: amazon.com):

- SanDisk Extreme microSDXC UHS-I 64 GB is priced at approximately $11.

2.1.4 Ethernet / LAN Cable

Figure 6 Ethernet Cable

A stable network and internet connection are essential for your Smart Home. Therefore, I recommend connecting the Raspberry Pi to your home network using Ethernet. When purchasing the Ethernet cable, ensure that it can transmit at least 1 gigabit. This should be the case for almost all Ethernet cables.

Estimated costs (as of October 2023, source: amazon.com):

- An Ethernet cable is priced at approximately $5-$10.

2.1.5 Z-Wave USB Dongle

Figure 7 Z-Wave USB Dongle

A Z-Wave USB stick allows you to seamlessly integrate Z-Wave devices into your Smart Home. Z-Wave is particularly suitable for controlling lights and blinds.

When researching your purchase, ensure that the Z-Wave USB dongle is compatible with your Raspberry Pi model (e.g., USB 2 / 3) and Smart Home system (e.g., Home Assistant).

Estimated costs (as of October 2023, source: amazon.com):

- A Z-Wave USB Dongle (e.g., Zooz 700) is priced at approximately $36.

2.1.6 Zigbee USB Dongle

Figure 8 Zigbee USB Dongle (schematic)

A Zigbee USB dongle allows the integration of Zigbee devices into your Raspberry Pi Smart Home. Zigbee is particularly suitable for the integration of lights, switches, and various sensors (such as temperature or window sensors).

When researching your purchase, ensure that the Zigbee USB dongle is compatible with your Raspberry Pi model (e.g., USB 2 / 3) and Smart Home system (e.g., Home Assistant).

Estimated costs (as of October 2023, source: amazon.com):

- The Phoscon ConBee II is priced at approximately $35.

2.1.7 Optional: Raspberry PI Case

The use of an optional Raspberry Pi case provides protection, stability, and improved aesthetics for your Raspberry Pi.

When researching your purchase, pay particular attention to compatibility with your chosen Raspberry Pi model.

Estimated costs (as of October 2023, source: amazon.com):

- The official Raspberry Pi 4 case is priced at approximately $10.

2.2 Recommended Devices for Your Smart Home

To control the devices in your home, you'll need suitable Smart Home components. I recommend the following components for this purpose:

- **Z-Wave modules** for controlling lights and blinds
  ➔ *as these can typically be installed behind your existing switches.*

- **Zigbee sensors** for monitoring windows, doors, and temperature,
  ➔ *as Zigbee sensors are affordable and readily available on the market, e.g., from Aqara.*

- **Philips Hue Bridge** for integrating Philips Hue devices,
  ➔ *as Hue devices are great for creating a pleasant ambiance, and the Hue Bridge simplifies integration.*

- **Amazon Alexa** for voice control of your Smart Home system,
  ➔ *as Alexa is easy to integrate and currently one of the best voice assistants on the market.*

- **Sonos** for voice output of notifications and music,
  ➔ *as Sonos speakers are easy to integrate and, in my opinion, offer excellent sound quality ;-).*

These components allow you to customize your Smart Home and utilize various functions.

2.2.1 Z-Wave Modules for Lighting and Blinds, for example

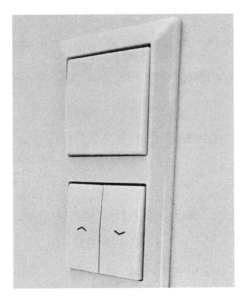

Figure 9 Z-Wave modules for lamps and blinds are typically installed behind switches

In the realm of Smart Home components, I recommend Z-Wave modules to enable various functions such as the control of lighting and blinds. These modules offer the following advantages:

- **Reliable Control**: Z-Wave modules allow you to control your lights and blinds reliably and precisely.

- **Expandability**: You can easily add more Z-Wave devices to expand your Smart Home system as needed.

- **Compatibility**: Z-Wave is a common standard compatible with a variety of Smart Home devices and systems.

- **Energy Efficiency**: Z-Wave technology enables efficient energy usage, leading to cost savings and environmentally friendly operation.

- **Security**: Z-Wave offers advanced security features to protect your data and Smart Home system.

With Z-Wave modules, you can easily and conveniently control the lighting and blinds in your Smart Home to enhance the ambiance and comfort in your home.

Estimated costs (as of October 2023, source: amazon.com):

- If you have dimmable lamps, you could consider the Zooz Dimmer ZEN31, which is priced at approximately $40. One dimmer is required per lamp.
- If you already have electronic blinds, you could opt for the Zooz 700 Series Z-Wave Relay ZEN17, priced at approximately $40. One relay is required per blind.

2.2.2 Zigbee Sensors for Windows, Doors, and Temperature

Figure 10 Aqara Temperature Sensor

Figure 11 Aqara Window/Door Sensor

For monitoring and controlling windows, doors, and temperature in your Smart Home, Zigbee sensors are recommended. These sensors offer several advantages:

- **Precise Detection**: Zigbee sensors allow for accurate detection of window and door status as well as temperature values.

- **Versatile Application**: You can use Zigbee sensors for both window and door monitoring and temperature measurement in various rooms.

- **Wireless Connectivity**: The sensors utilize wireless Zigbee technology, enabling easy installation and wireless communication with other Smart Home devices.

- **Expandability**: You can easily add more Zigbee sensors to expand the monitoring capabilities of your Smart Home system.

- **Compatibility**: Zigbee is a widespread standard compatible with a variety of Smart Home devices and systems.

By integrating Zigbee sensors into your Smart Home system, you gain reliable monitoring and control over windows, doors, and temperature. This allows you to enhance the security, comfort, and energy efficiency in your home.

Estimated costs (as of October 2023, source: amazon.com):

- An Aqara door and window sensor is priced at approximately $18.
- An Aqara temperature and humidity sensor is priced at approximately $20.

2.2.3   Philips Hue Bridge for Hue Integration

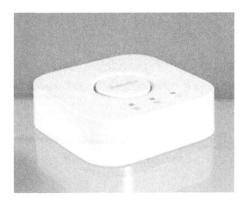

Figure 12 Hue Bridge

For seamless integration of Philips Hue devices into your Smart Home, it is recommended to use a Hue Bridge. This bridge can be later integrated into Home Assistant.

The integration of the Hue Bridge into your Smart Home system enables comprehensive control and personalization of your lighting. You can adjust the brightness, color, and mood of the lamps and create various lighting scenarios for different activities. This creates an inviting and comfortable atmosphere in your home.

Since Hue devices use the Zigbee protocol, theoretically, we could forego the Hue Bridge by using our Zigbee USB stick to integrate Hue devices. However, if you plan to integrate Hue devices into your Smart Home, I would recommend also purchasing a Hue Bridge, as it enhances Smart Home convenience and facilitates device integration.

Estimated costs (as of October 2023, source: amazon.com):

- A Philips Hue Bridge is priced at approximately $46.

2.2.4 Amazon Alexa for Voice Control

Figure 13 Amazon Echo with Alexa

Using Amazon Alexa for voice control of your Smart Home offers numerous benefits and possibilities. Here are some reasons why Amazon Alexa is a recommended option:

- **Voice-Controlled Operation**: With Amazon Alexa, you can conveniently control your Smart Home via voice commands. By integrating Alexa into your Smart Home system, you can activate and control various devices and functions with your voice.

- **Personalized Automation**: With Amazon Alexa, you can create customized scenes and routines to perform specific actions in your Smart Home. For example, you can create a "Good Night" routine that automatically turns off all lights, locks the door, and activates the alarm when you say, "Good night, Alexa."

- **Third-Party Service Integration**: Amazon Alexa offers a wide range of skills and third-party integrations. You can stream music, retrieve information, create shopping lists, get weather reports, and more, simply by speaking to Alexa.

Integrating Amazon Alexa into your Smart Home enables intuitive and convenient control of your devices and functions. You can personalize your home by activating various actions and scenes using voice commands. With Alexa as your voice assistant, operating your Smart Home becomes even easier and more comfortable.

Estimated costs (as of October 2023, source: amazon.com):

- An Amazon Echo Dot is priced at approximately $23.

2.2.5 Sonos for Voice Output and Music

Figure 14 Sonos One Speaker

Sonos provides a premium solution for voice output and music playback in your Smart Home. Here are some reasons why Sonos is a recommended option for these functions:

- **Versatile Audio Playback**: With Sonos, you can play music, podcasts, and other audio content in high quality in various rooms of your home. You can create individual speakers or groups of speakers to enjoy synchronized audio playback throughout your home.

- **Integrated Voice Control**: Sonos supports popular voice assistants like Amazon Alexa and Google Assistant. This allows you to control your Sonos speakers by voice, play music, adjust the volume, and more. Voice control integration offers convenient music playback control.

- **Multiroom Functionality**: With Sonos, you can connect different speakers in your Smart Home to create a multiroom audio system. This enables you to play music simultaneously in various rooms or play different content in different areas. This flexibility allows you to create the right atmosphere in your home.

- **Easy Integration into Your Smart Home**: Sonos seamlessly integrates with other Smart Home platforms and devices. You can integrate your Sonos speakers into your Smart Home system and link them seamlessly with other devices and automations. For example, you can set up music to play automatically when you arrive home or when your alarm system is triggered.

With Sonos as your voice output and music solution in your Smart Home, you can enjoy an immersive audio experience and seamlessly control your music playback. The versatility, voice control, and integration into your Smart Home make Sonos a recommended option for high-quality audio playback.

Note: While the integrated Alexa voice control in Sonos speakers is suitable for calling Smart Home commands, searching for, and integrating Smart Home devices requires an original Amazon Echo.

Estimated costs (as of October 2023, source: amazon.com):

- A Sonos One speaker starts at approximately $300.

2.3 Cost Calculation

To determine the total costs for the Smart Home Hub and Smart Home devices, we will sum up the individual cost components:

Smart Home Hub:

- Raspberry Pi: approximately $52 - $66

- Raspberry Pi Power Supply: approximately $15-20

- SanDisk microSD Card: approximately $11

- Ethernet Cable: approximately $5 - $10

- Z-Wave USB Stick: approximately $36

- Phoscon ConBee II: approximately $35

- Raspberry Pi Case: approximately $10

Total cost for the Smart Home Hub: approximately $164 - $188

Smart Home Devices:

- Zooz Dimmer ZEN31 (per lamp): approximately $40

- Zooz 700 Series Z-Wave Relay ZEN17 (per roller shutter): approximately $40

- Aqara Door and Window Sensor: approximately $18

- Aqara Temperature and Humidity Sensor: approximately $20

- Philips Hue Bridge: approximately $46

- Amazon Echo Dot: approximately $23

- Sonos One Speaker: starting at approximately $300

The total costs for Smart Home devices vary depending on individual needs and can vary significantly.

Example total costs for 4 dimmers, 8 roller shutters, 8 door and window sensors, 4 temperature and humidity sensors, 1 Hue Bridge, and 1 Echo Dot: approximately $773.

2.4 Hardware Setup

You've obtained all the components for your Smart Home Hub and your Smart Home? Great, let's get started with the hardware setup. This is a crucial step for your Smart Home project. In this chapter, we'll cover setting up the Raspberry Pi Smart Home Hub and equipping your apartment or house with Smart Home devices.

You'll learn how to properly configure the Raspberry Pi Smart Home Hub and where to place components in your apartment or house to optimize your Smart Home system. A careful hardware setup lays the foundation for an effective and smoothly functioning Smart Home system.

2.4.1   Raspberry Pi Smart Home Hub Setup

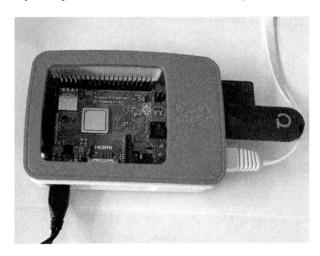

Figure 15 Raspberry Pi Smart Home Hub

Setting up your Raspberry Pi Smart Home Hub requires several components that need to be carefully assembled and installed. Follow these steps to set up your Smart Home Hub:

1. **Raspberry Pi**: Start with a Raspberry Pi 3 or 4 to serve as the foundation for your Smart Home Hub.

2. **Raspberry Pi Case**: Place the Raspberry Pi in a suitable case to protect it from external influences. Ensure that the case provides adequate ventilation to prevent overheating.

Figure 16 Raspberry Pi in Case

3. **Zigbee Stick**: Insert the Zigbee USB stick into one of the Raspberry Pi's USB ports. This allows communication with Zigbee-enabled sensors and devices.

4. **Z-Wave Stick**: Add the Z-Wave USB stick into another USB port of the Raspberry Pi. This enables interaction with Z-Wave devices such as lights and blinds.

Figure 17 Zigbee- und Z-Wave-Stick in Raspberry Pi

5. **SD Card**: Insert the micro SD card into the corresponding card slot of the Raspberry Pi.

Figure 18 SD Card in Raspberry Pi

6. **Wiring**: Connect the Raspberry Pi to your home network using an Ethernet cable to establish a reliable network connection.

7. **Power Supply**: Connect the supplied power adapter to the Raspberry Pi to ensure power is provided.

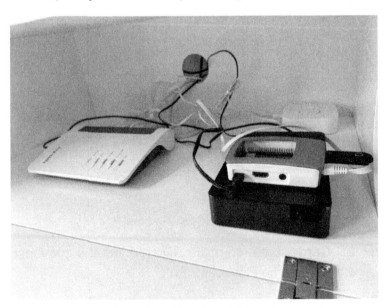

Figure 19 Operational Raspberry Pi Smart Home Hub

Once you've completed these steps, your Raspberry Pi Smart Home Hub is ready on the hardware side. However, you still need to install the Smart Home software "Home Assistant" on the SD card, which will be covered in Chapter 3.

2.4.2 Equipping Your Apartment or House with Smart Home Components

Equipping your apartment or house with Smart Home components offers you a multitude of automation and control possibilities. Here are some recommendations and guidelines for installation:

1. **Z-Wave Dimmers and Blinds Controls**: These components enable remote control and regulation of lights and blinds. Due to electrical installation, it is recommended to have these installed or checked by a qualified electrician to ensure correct and safe installation.

2. **Zigbee Sensors**: Zigbee sensors are easy to mount and typically attach using adhesive materials. You can place them on every window and door, especially the front door. Additionally, you can use temperature sensors to monitor room temperature. Installing these sensors usually does not require special expertise and can be done by yourself.

3. **Amazon Alexa**: To use voice control in your Smart Home, you can set up an Amazon Alexa device. The setup is simple and only requires a connection to the Wi-Fi network.

4. **Sonos Speakers**: If you want to enjoy music throughout your house, Sonos speakers are ideal for music playback. Place the speakers in strategic locations to ensure optimal sound quality in different rooms.

5. **Philips Hue Lights**: Philips Hue lights are excellent for ambient lighting in your apartment. You can opt for Hue Lightstrips (indoor and outdoor), for example. For securing the Outdoor Lightstrips, I would recommend using U-profiles (plastic is sufficient) from the hardware store. For securing the Indoor Lightstrips, I would also recommend using

specialized adhesive tape, available at the hardware store. It's best to inquire with the hardware store staff about the most suitable tape for this purpose. The Philips Hue lights can later be controlled via the Hue app and also through Home Assistant.

Note that the exact installation and configuration of individual components may vary from manufacturer to manufacturer. Therefore, always consult the provided manuals and guides to ensure you install and operate the devices correctly.

2.5 Troubleshooting and Common Issues

Setting up and using a Smart Home can lead to various problems. Here are some common issues and recommendations for solving them:

1. **Connectivity Problems**: Ensure that the devices are within the network's range, and there are no obstacles blocking signals. Also, check the network connection and router settings.

2. **Compatibility Issues**: Verify the compatibility of the devices and update firmware or software if necessary.

3. **Incorrect Configuration**: Review the settings and configurations of the Smart Home Hub and the devices.

4. **Power Supply Problems**: Ensure a stable power supply and use appropriate power adapters.

5. **Missing Updates**: Perform regular updates to fix issues and improve performance.

Consult the user manuals, support documentation, and technical support of the manufacturers for specific solutions.

If you encounter a different issue and can't find a solution despite internet research, feel free to reach out to me at info@rothech.com. I am happy to assist.

2.6 Summary

In Chapter 2, we discussed the recommended hardware configuration for your Smart Home. We introduced a variety of components suitable for building a Smart Home Hub and equipping your apartment or house.

First, we discussed the recommended components for your Smart Home Hub, including the Raspberry Pi 3 or 4, the power supply, the micro SD card, the SD card reader, the Ethernet cable, and extensions such as Z-Wave and Zigbee USB sticks, and a Raspberry Pi case.

Next, we introduced the recommended components for your Smart Home, including Z-Wave modules for lighting and blinds control, Zigbee sensors for windows, doors, and temperature, the Hue Bridge for integrating Hue lights, Amazon Alexa for voice control, and Sonos for voice output and music playback.

The total cost for the Smart Home Hub is approximately 135 euros, while the cost for the example with various devices is approximately 1,019 euros (for 4 dimmers, 8 roller shutters, 8 door and window sensors, 4 temperature sensors, one Hue Bridge, and one Echo Dot).

Later in the chapter, we covered the hardware setup, including setting up the Raspberry Pi Smart Home Hub and installing Z-Wave dimmers and blinds controls. We emphasized that it's best to have an electrician handle the installation of these devices, while mounting Zigbee sensors is typically a straightforward DIY task.

Finally, we addressed troubleshooting and common issues. Here, we discussed various problems such as connectivity issues, compatibility problems, incorrect configurations, power supply issues, and missing updates, providing recommendations for solutions.

With this comprehensive knowledge of the recommended hardware configuration and Smart Home equipment, you are now well-prepared to successfully set up and use your own Smart Home.

3 Home Assistant Setup

Chapter three focuses on setting up Home Assistant, a powerful smart home platform. Here, you will learn how to install Home Assistant, use its basic features, and troubleshoot potential issues. Additionally, important aspects like automated backups and remote access will be covered.

3.1 Introduction to Home Assistant

Figure 20 Home Assistant Logo

Home Assistant is an open-source platform for smart home automation that offers numerous advantages over other systems. With Home Assistant, you have the ability to seamlessly integrate various devices and services, customizing your smart home to your preferences.

Some of the benefits of Home Assistant include:

1. **Open and flexible platform**: Thanks to the open-source nature of Home Assistant and its active community, there are a variety of integrations and extensions available. You can incorporate different brands, protocols, and devices into your system, providing you with maximum flexibility.

2. **Local processing**: Unlike cloud-based smart home systems, Home Assistant runs locally on your own server or Raspberry Pi. This allows you to retain full control over your data and remain independent of a stable internet connection or cloud server failures.

3. **Vendor independence**: Home Assistant allows you to choose and combine various devices and services independently. You are not tied to a specific manufacturer or provider and can select components that suit your needs.

4. **Automation flexibility**: Home Assistant offers extensive automation features, allowing you to create complex scenarios and workflows. You can configure triggers, conditions, and actions to intelligently control your smart home to meet your needs.

5. **Extensibility**: Home Assistant can be further customized and extended through add-ons and extensions. The community continuously develops new integrations that allow you to incorporate new devices and services into your system.

With Home Assistant, you gain a powerful and flexible platform for managing and automating your smart home. The multitude of integrations, local processing, vendor independence, automation flexibility, and extensibility make Home Assistant an attractive choice for smart home enthusiasts.

3.2 Installing Home Assistant OS

Installing Home Assistant OS on a Raspberry Pi SD card involves several steps:

Step 1: Write Image to Your SD Card

1. Download the **Raspberry Pi Imager** from the official website and install it on your computer. You can find it at https://www.raspberrypi.com/software/.

2. Open the Raspberry Pi Imager and select the **operating system**:

   • Choose "**Choose OS**"

- Select "**Other specific-purpose OS** > **Home assistants and home automation** > **Home Assistant**"

- Choose the appropriate **Home Assistant OS** for your **hardware** (**RPi 3 or RPi 4**).

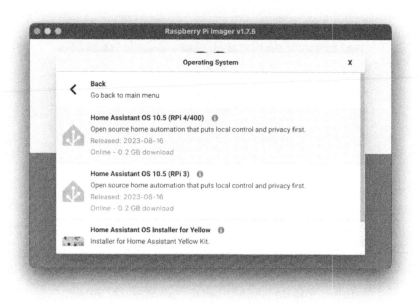

Figure 21 Raspberry Pi Imager - Home Assistant OS

3. Insert the **SD card** into your computer's SD card reader.

4. Select your **SD card** by selecting "Choose Storage".

Figure 22 Home Assistant – Choose Storage

5. Start the writing process by clicking "**Write**"

6. **Wait** until Home Assistant OS is written to the SD card.

7. **Safely remove the SD card** from your computer.

Step 2: Boot Up Your Raspberry Pi

1. Assemble your **Raspberry Pi smart home hub**. You can find instructions in Chapter 2.4.1. *Note: The power supply should not be connected at this stage.*

2. Insert the **SD card** into your **Raspberry Pi** and make sure that the **ethernet cable** is connected.

3. Connect the **power supply** to start the device.

4. Open the **web browser** on your desktop system.

5. **After a few minutes**, you can access your new Home

Assistant via http://homeassistant.local:8123. You should see the following window:

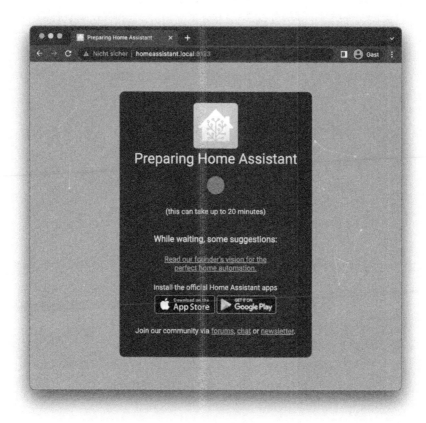

Figure 23 Home Assistant Installation on Raspberry Pi

Note: If http://homeassistant.local:8123 is not accessible even after several minutes, you may need to access Home Assistant via http://X.X.X.X:8123, replacing X.X.X.X with the IP address of your Raspberry Pi.

Congratulations! You have successfully installed Home Assistant on your Raspberry Pi. With the Home Assistant Operating System installed and accessible, you can now proceed with the setup.

3.3 Getting Started with Home Assistant

Congratulations, you've made it! The most challenging part is behind you. Now it's time to take the first steps with Home Assistant.

After entering the address of your Home Assistant device into your browser's address bar, the setup screen will appear. Depending on your hardware, the setup might take some time.

With Home Assistant installed, it's time to set up the basics:

1. **Create your user account:**
   - Enter a name, username, and password.
   - Select "Create Account" to create the account.
2. **Define the settings:**
   - Enter a name for your home.
   - Choose location-specific settings and the language for the user interface.
   - You can either automatically set the settings or enter them manually.
3. **Share your information (optional):**
   - Choose what information you are willing to share.
   - Data sharing is disabled by default.
   - Once you're done, select "Next."
4. **Discover devices on your network:**
   - Home Assistant will then display all the devices it has discovered on your network.
   - Don't worry if you see fewer devices than expected; you can manually add more devices later.
   - You don't need to configure devices at this stage. We'll do that later.
   - Select "Finish," and you will be redirected to the Home Assistant Dashboard. Here, you will see all the devices you selected.

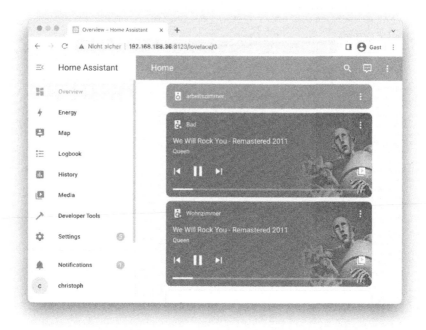

Figure 24 Initial Home Assistant Dashboard (with example devices)

You have now successfully taken the first steps with Home Assistant and can begin configuring and automating your smart home.

3.4 Overview of Home Assistant Functionality

Now that you're in Home Assistant, let's take a closer look at its essential components and understand what they do. These can be configured via the "Settings" menu.

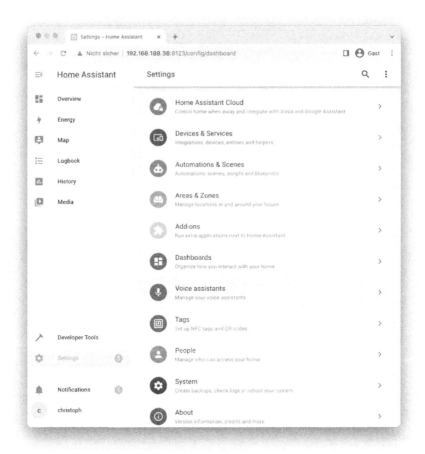

Figure 25 Overview of Home Assistant Functionality

1. **Dashboards**: Dashboards are customizable pages displaying information connected to Home Assistant and available within Home Assistant. By default, there are two dashboards: "Overview" and "Energy." The Overview Dashboard is the first one you see after the onboarding process. Here, you can find more details.

2. **Integrations**: Integrations are software components that allow Home Assistant to connect with other platforms. For example, the Philips Hue product uses the Philips Hue Integration to connect Home Assistant to the Hue Bridge

hardware controller. All devices connected to the Hue Bridge and compatible with Home Assistant will appear in Home Assistant as devices. You can find a complete list of compatible integrations here.

3. **Devices & Entities**: Devices are a logical grouping of one or more entities. A device can represent a physical device, which, in turn, can have one or more sensors. These sensors are connected to the device as entities. For example, a motion sensor can be represented as a device, while motion detection, temperature, and light levels are associated entities. Entities have states like "on" for motion detection and "off" when there's no motion. Devices and entities are used in various areas of Home Assistant:

   - Dashboards display the state of an entity, such as whether a light bulb is on or off, and buttons for interacting with devices, like turning a light bulb on or off.

   - Automations can be triggered by changes in entity states and control other devices or entities.

   - Scenes allow you to save preset settings for devices and recall them when needed.

4. **Automations**: Automations are collections of repeatable actions that can be automatically executed. An automation consists of three main components:

   - Triggers: Events that initiate an automation, such as a sunset event.

   - Conditions (optional): Tests that must be met before actions are executed. For example, a condition might require someone to be at home.

   - Actions: Interactions with devices, such as turning

on a lamp.

5. **Scripts**: Scripts are similar to automations in that they involve repeatable actions, but they do not have their own triggers. This means scripts are not automatically executed unless used within an automation. Scripts can be useful when you want to repeat the same actions in various automations or trigger them from a dashboard.

6. **Scenes**: Scenes allow you to create preset settings for your devices. Similar to driving modes on smartphones or driver profiles in cars, scenes customize the environment to your needs. For example, a movie-watching scene might include dimmed lights, a turned-on TV, and increased volume. These settings can be saved as a scene and easily recalled without manually adjusting each device every time.

7. **Add-Ons**: Depending on your installation type, you may have the option to install third-party add-ons. Add-ons are typically apps compatible with Home Assistant that offer a quick and easy way to integrate additional functionalities into Home Assistant.

By understanding these key functionalities of Home Assistant, you are well-prepared to harness the full potential of the system. In the following chapters, we will delve into more advanced topics and explore the capabilities of Home Assistant in greater depth.

3.5 Setting Up an Automatic Backup

Automated daily backups of Home Assistant are essential to ensure you always have access to a functioning version in case something goes wrong. In this chapter, we will show you how to set up an automated backup using the "Home Assistant Google Drive Backup" add-on.

Step 1: Install the "Home Assistant Google Drive Backup" Add-

On Repository

- Go to the **Add-On Store** in the Home Assistant interface. You can find this under "Settings" > "Add-ons" > "Add-on Store" (bottom-right blue button).

- Click on the three dots "..." in the upper right and select **"Repositories."**

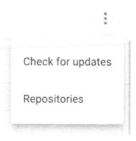

Figure 26 Add-on Repositories Menu

- In the text box, enter the following address and then click **"Add"**: https://github.com/sabeechen/hassio-google-drive-backup

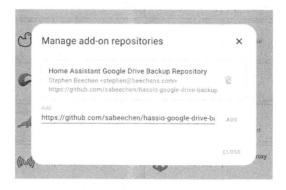

Figure 27 Add-On Repository Addition

- Click **"Close"** when finished.

Step 2: Install the "Home Assistant Google Drive Backup" Add-On

- Go to the Add-On Store in the Home Assistant interface.

- Search for "Home Assistant Google Drive Backup" and install it. Click on the search result, then press the "Install" button.

- Start the add-on by clicking "Start."

Step 3: Configure the Add-On

- Open the configuration for the "Home Assistant Google Drive Backup" add-on. You can access the configuration interface by clicking "Open Web UI" on the add-on page.

- Click "Authenticate with Drive" and sign in with your Google Account.

- Set the schedule for automatic backups.

Step 4: Start the Backup

- Click "Start" or "Backup Now" to manually start the backup.

Step 5: Check the Backup Status

- Check the status of the backup in the log section of the add-on.

Step 6: Verify Your Google Drive Account

- Open your Google Drive account and check the backup folder.

With an automated backup of Home Assistant, you are protected against potential data loss and can always revert to a working version.

3.6 Remote Access via VPN

Remote access to your Home Assistant system allows you to

control your smart home environment from anywhere. This chapter will guide you on setting up a secure remote access to Home Assistant by using VPN directly in your router settings.

Step 1: Check VPN Support

- Check if your router supports VPN.

- Ensure that your router supports the necessary VPN protocols, such as OpenVPN or IPsec.

Step 2: Configure VPN in the Router

- Access your router settings.

- Navigate to the VPN menu or advanced settings.

- Enable the VPN feature and select the desired VPN protocol.

Step 3: Set Up VPN Connection

- Input the necessary information for the VPN service, such as server address, username, and password.

- Save the VPN configuration.

Step 4: Establish Connection

- Connect your external device (e.g., laptop or smartphone) to a different network.

- Activate the VPN connection on your device and select the corresponding server.

Step 5: Test Remote Access

- Open a web browser and enter the local IP address of your Home Assistant server.

- Verify if you can successfully access the Home Assistant

user interface.

Setting up VPN directly in your router settings allows you to establish a secure connection to your Home Assistant system from any location. However, note that VPN configuration may vary from router to router. Consult your router's user manual or contact the manufacturer for specific instructions.

3.7 Troubleshooting and Common Issues

This chapter addresses common problems when using Home Assistant and provides solutions for these difficulties. If you encounter issues, you'll find helpful tips and tricks to resolve them here.

Problem 1: Home Assistant Doesn't Start Properly

- Restart the Raspberry Pi by disconnecting and reconnecting the power supply (only as a last resort, as this may affect your smart home operating system).

- If all else fails, reinstall Home Assistant or restore a backup.

Problem 2: Connection Issues with the Home Assistant User Interface

- Ensure that your device is connected to the same network as the Home Assistant server.

- Check the IP address and port to ensure you're using the correct information.

- Verify firewall settings.

Problem 3: Faulty User Interface or Missing Information

- Clear the browser cache and reload the page.

- Check the configuration of the user interface and views.

- Update Home Assistant to the latest version.

Problem 4: Connection Issues with External Services or Devices

- Check the network connection and accessibility of external services or devices.

- Ensure that access credentials and configurations are entered correctly.

- Update the firmware or software of external devices.

For persistent issues you can't resolve, I recommend using the Home Assistant community forums and resources. There, you'll find an active community of users who can assist with troubleshooting and finding solutions.

If you encounter a different issue and can't find a solution despite internet research, feel free to reach out to me at info@rothech.com. I am happy to assist.

3.8 Summary

In this chapter, we have covered the key aspects of setting up and using Home Assistant. Here is a summary of the topics addressed:

Introduction to Home Assistant:

- Home Assistant is an open-source platform for smart homes and home automation.
- It provides a central interface for controlling and automating various devices and services.

Installation of Home Assistant:

- Home Assistant OS can be easily installed on your SD card using the Raspberry Pi Imager.

Getting Started with Home Assistant:

- After installation, set up your user account and configure basic settings like location and language.

Overview of Home Assistant Functionalities:

- Dashboards allow viewing and controlling information and devices in Home Assistant.
- Integrations connect Home Assistant with various devices and services.
- Devices and entities represent physical and logical units in Home Assistant.
- Automations, scripts, and scenes enable automation of actions and settings in Home Assistant.
- Add-ons expand the functionality of Home Assistant with additional applications and services.

Setting Up Automated Backups:

- Regularly backing up your Home Assistant configuration is crucial to prevent data loss.
- The Home Assistant Google Drive Backup Add-on enables automatic backup of your configuration to Google Drive.

Remote Access via VPN:

- Setting up a VPN allows secure remote access to your Home Assistant server over the internet.
- If your router has integrated VPN settings, you can configure remote access directly through it.

Troubleshooting and Common Issues:

- Various troubleshooting methods, including configuration checks, reboots, and updates, can help resolve problems.
- Community forums and resources offer support for troubleshooting and finding solutions.

With this knowledge, you are well-equipped to successfully set up and use Home Assistant. You can personalize your smart home, create automations, and centrally manage your devices. Don't be discouraged by occasional challenges and make the most of the diverse opportunities that Home Assistant provides. In the next chapter, you will learn how to integrate your smart home devices with Z-Wave and Zigbee.

4 Integrating Z-Wave and Zigbee in Home Assistant

In this chapter, we will focus on integrating Z-Wave and Zigbee into Home Assistant. Here, you'll learn how to set up and configure Z-Wave and Zigbee.

4.1 Integrating Z-Wave

4.1.1 Introduction to Z-Wave

Figure 28 Z-Wave Dongle

What is Z-Wave?

Z-Wave is a wireless communication protocol designed specifically for home automation. It enables wireless communication between various devices in your smart home. With Z-Wave, you can control and automate your lighting, heating, security systems, and more.

Benefits of Z-Wave

Z-Wave offers a variety of benefits for your smart home. Here are some of the key advantages:

1. **Reliable Communication**: Z-Wave uses a mesh network structure where each device acts as a repeater, ensuring reliable and stable communication, even in larger living spaces.

2. **Easy Installation**: Setting up Z-Wave devices is typically

straightforward and uncomplicated. You can easily add new devices and connect them to your Z-Wave network.

3. **Interoperability**: Z-Wave is an open standard supported by many different manufacturers, allowing you to seamlessly integrate a wide range of devices from different brands into your Z-Wave network.

4. **Security**: Z-Wave employs advanced security features such as encrypted communication to ensure the privacy and security of your data.

Z-Wave Components

To use Z-Wave in your smart home, you need some basic components:

1. **Z-Wave Hub**: A Z-Wave hub is the heart of your Z-Wave network. It serves as the central control unit that facilitates communication between Z-Wave devices. In this book, we use a Z-Wave USB stick as a Z-Wave hub.

2. **Z-Wave Devices**: These are the actual devices you want to control in your smart home. They can include various types of devices, such as light switches, outlets, thermostats, door locks, and sensors.

3. **Z-Wave Network**: The Z-Wave network consists of the hub and the Z-Wave devices that communicate with each other. It forms the foundation for controlling and automating your smart home.

4.2 Setting Up Z-Wave in Home Assistant

Setting up Z-Wave in Home Assistant allows for a seamless integration of your Z-Wave devices into your smart home system. In this chapter, we'll guide you through the step-by-step process of setting up Z-Wave in Home Assistant.

Step 1: Preparation

- Ensure that you have connected the Z-Wave USB stick to your Raspberry Pi.

Step 2: Activate Z-Wave Integration

- Open the Home Assistant user interface, go to the Settings, and select "Devices & Services."

- Here, you should find your Z-Wave stick under "Integration."

- Click the "Configure" button for your Z-Wave stick and click "Submit" on the following popup.

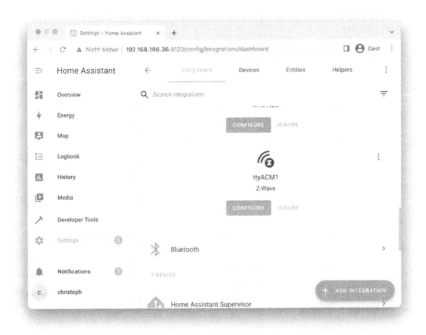

Figure 29 Configure Z-Wave Stick

Step 3: Configure the Z-Wave Network

- Follow the instructions to configure the network settings and integrate the controller into the network.

- You will see a dialogue stating that Z-Wave is now being installed.

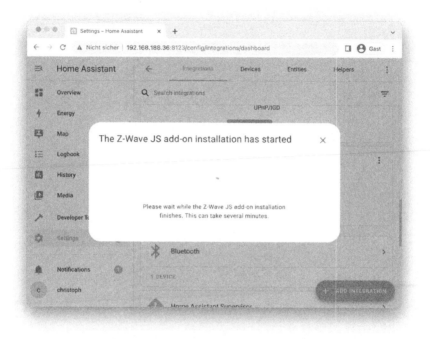

Figure 30 Z-Wave-JS Add-on is being installed

- You can then enter custom keys. This step can be skipped by clicking "Submit."

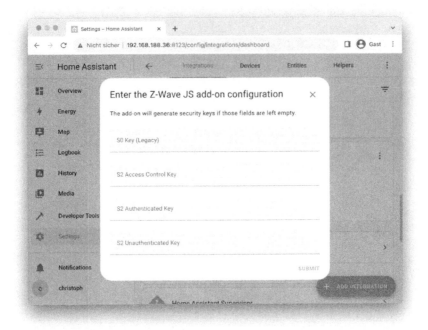

Figure 31 Z-Wave Keys

- Next, the Z-Wave add-on will be started.

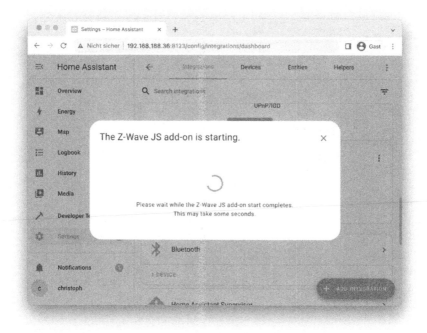

Figure 32 Start of Z-Wave Add-on

- You'll receive confirmation that the configuration was successful.

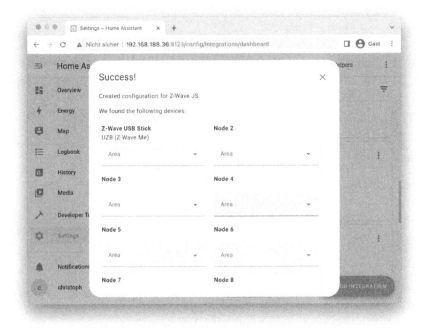

Figure 33 Z-Wave successfully configured[1]

Step 5: Add Devices

- Once your Z-Wave network is configured, you can add your Z-Wave devices.

- Navigate to the Z-Wave integration view, located under Settings -> Devices & Services -> Integrations -> Click on "zwave_js."

---

[1] Here, you probably only see the Z-Wave stick at your place.

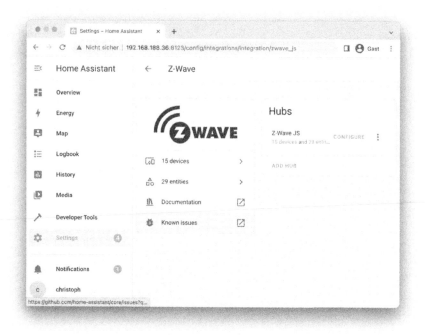

Figure 34 Z-Wave Integration View

- Click the "Configure" button next to "Z-Wave JS" under "Hubs."

- Then, click the "Add Device" button at the bottom right.

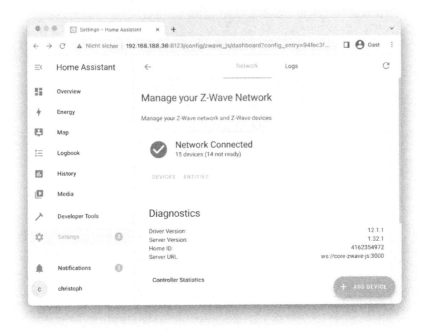

Figure 35 Add Z-Wave Device

- Follow the instructions to include specific Z-Wave devices in your network.

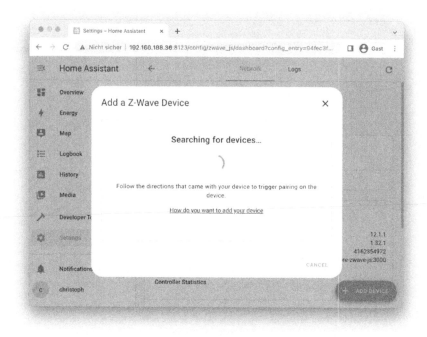

Figure 36 Z-Wave Device Search

Step 6: Verification and Testing

- After successfully adding your Z-Wave devices, verify their functionality in Home Assistant.

- Test controlling the devices and monitor their status changes to ensure everything works smoothly.

- Simply navigate to the device you added, for example, under "Settings" -> "Devices & Services" -> "Devices" -> click on the Z-Wave device in the list.

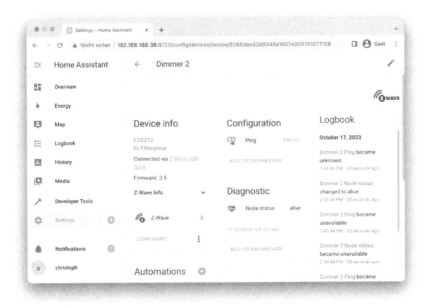

Figure 37 Z-Wave Device View

With Z-Wave successfully set up in Home Assistant, you now have the ability to seamlessly integrate your Z-Wave devices into your smart home and utilize extensive automation and control options.

4.3 Integrating Zigbee in Home Assistant

4.3.1 Introduction to Zigbee

Figure 38 Phoscon ConBee II Zigbee USB Stick

Zigbee is a wireless communication protocol specifically designed for home automation, allowing you to control and automate a variety of devices in your smart home.

What is Zigbee?

Zigbee is a wireless protocol designed for communication in smart homes. It is based on the IEEE 802.15.4 standard and is known for its reliability, energy efficiency, and ease of use. Zigbee enables seamless integration and control of various devices, including light switches, outlets, thermostats, door locks, sensors, and more.

Benefits of Zigbee:

- **Reliable Communication**: Zigbee utilizes a mesh network where each Zigbee device acts as a repeater, ensuring robust and reliable communication, even in larger living spaces.

- **Easy Installation**: Zigbee devices are typically easy to integrate into your smart home. The setup is done through the Zigbee hub, which serves as the central control unit.

- **Interoperability**: Zigbee is an open standard supported by various manufacturers. This allows you to seamlessly integrate Zigbee devices from different brands into your Zigbee network and combine various functionalities.

- **Energy Efficiency**: Zigbee devices are designed to operate efficiently, providing extended battery life. This saves energy and reduces the frequency of battery replacement.

Components of Zigbee:

- **Zigbee Hub:** The Zigbee hub is the core of your Zigbee network, acting as the central control unit that facilitates communication between Zigbee devices. In this book, we use a Zigbee USB stick as the Zigbee hub.

- **Zigbee Devices:** These are the actual devices you want to control and automate in your smart home, such as light switches, outlets, thermostats, door locks, motion sensors, and more.

- **Zigbee Network:** The Zigbee network consists of the hub and Zigbee devices that communicate with each other. It forms the basis for controlling and automating your smart home.

4.3.2   Setting Up Zigbee in Home Assistant

Setting up Zigbee in Home Assistant enables a seamless integration of your Zigbee devices into your smart home system. In this section, we'll guide you through the step-by-step process of setting up Zigbee in Home Assistant.

Step 1: Preparation

- Ensure that you have connected the Zigbee USB stick to your Raspberry Pi.

Step 2: Activate the Zigbee Integration

- Open the Home Assistant user interface, go to the Settings, and select "Devices & Services."

- Under "Integrations," you should find your Zigbee stick.

- Click the "Configure" button for your Zigbee stick.

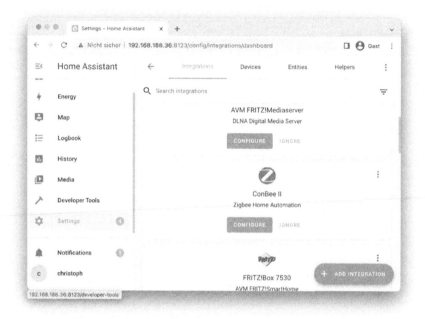

Figure 39 Zigbee Stick in Settings

Step 3: Configure the Zigbee Network

- After clicking the "Configure" button, follow the configuration steps for Zigbee.

- Follow the instructions for configuring network settings and integrating the hub into the network.

  - Confirm the prompt "Do you want to set up ConBee II?" with the "Submit" button.

  - In the subsequent dialogue, choose "Keep network settings" or "Delete network settings and build a new network" as needed.

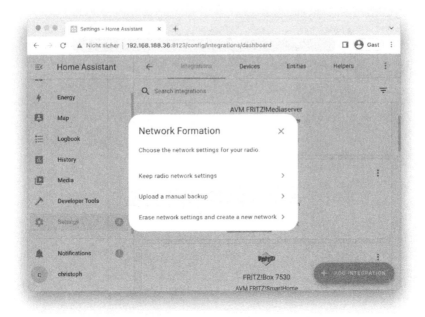

Figure 40 Zigbee Integration Configuration

Step 5: Add Devices

- Once your Zigbee network is configured, you can add your Zigbee devices.

- Navigate to the "Zigbee Home Automation" view under "Settings" -> "Devices & Services" -> Click on "Zigbee Home Automation."

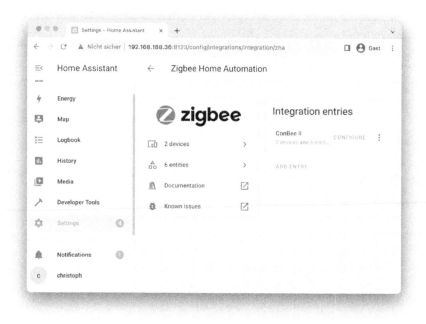

Figure 41 Zigbee Home Automation View

- In the "Zigbee Home Automation Overview," click "Configure" next to your Zigbee stick (ConBee II).

- Then, click the blue "Add Device" button at the bottom right.

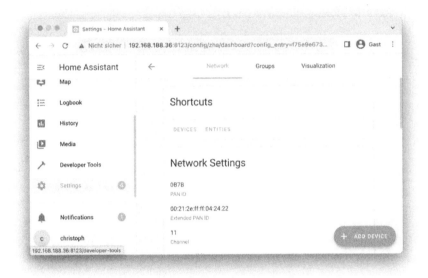

Figure 42 Add Zigbee Device

- Your Zigbee devices will be searched for in the vicinity.

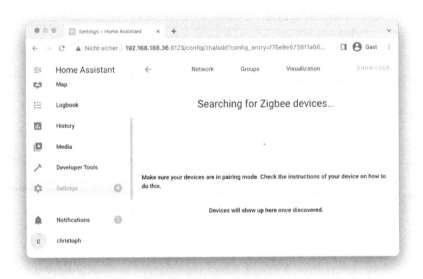

Figure 43 Searching for Zigbee Devices

- Follow the instructions to include specific Zigbee devices in your network.

- If your Zigbee device is successfully found, you will receive the message "The device is ready." You can also assign a readable name to the device at this point.

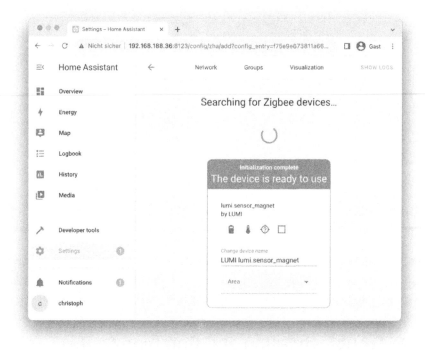

Figure 44 Zigbee Device is ready

Step 6: Verification and Testing

- After successfully adding your Zigbee devices, verify their functionality in Home Assistant.

- Test controlling the devices and monitor their status changes to ensure everything works smoothly.

- Navigate to the device you added, for example, under "Settings" -> "Devices & Services" -> "Devices" -> click on the Zigbee device in the list.

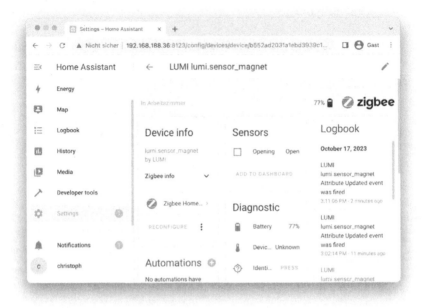

Figure 45 Zigbee Device View

With Zigbee successfully set up in Home Assistant, you now have the ability to seamlessly integrate your Zigbee devices into your smart home and utilize extensive automation and control options.

4.4 Troubleshooting and Common Issues

In this chapter, we address common problems when using Zigbee and Z-Wave in Home Assistant and provide solutions for these challenges. If you encounter issues, you'll find helpful tips and tricks to resolve them.

Problem 1: Zigbee or Z-Wave Devices Are Not Detected or Are Not Functioning Properly

- Check if your Zigbee or Z-Wave hub is properly connected to the Home Assistant host.

- Ensure that the Zigbee or Z-Wave devices have been correctly included in the network.

- Check the range of the devices and consider placing them closer to the hub or adding repeaters to extend the network.

Problem 2: Connection Issues Between the Hub and Devices

- Verify the battery performance of Zigbee or Z-Wave devices and replace batteries if necessary.

- Check for interference from other wireless devices that may disrupt the signal.

- Perform a network scan to identify potential sources of interference and take appropriate actions.

Problem 3: Zigbee or Z-Wave Devices Respond with Delays or Do Not Show Status Updates

- Check the positioning of the hub to ensure it is near the devices.

- Examine whether there is network congestion and, if necessary, reduce the number of concurrently active devices.

- Update the firmware of both the hub and the devices to address potential issues.

Problem 4: Network Range Issues

- Place repeaters or range extenders strategically to expand the network range.

- Use external antennas or signal boosters to enhance the signal strength of the hubs.

For persistent issues you can't resolve, I recommend using the Home Assistant community forums and resources. There, you'll find an active community of users who can assist with troubleshooting and finding solutions.

If you encounter a different issue and can't find a solution despite internet research, feel free to reach out to me at info@rothech.com. I am happy to assist.

4.5 Summary

In this chapter, we delved into the integration of Zigbee and Z-Wave in Home Assistant. We explained the basic concepts and advantages of these wireless communication protocols and provided step-by-step guides for setting them up in Home Assistant.

Zigbee is an open standard that enables reliable and energy-efficient communication between various smart home devices. By integrating Zigbee into Home Assistant, you can incorporate a wide range of Zigbee devices such as light switches, sensors, and thermostats into your smart home.

Z-Wave is a wireless protocol specifically designed for home automation, providing stable and secure communication between devices and allowing you to control and automate your lighting, heating, security systems, and more.

Setting up Zigbee and Z-Wave in Home Assistant requires the appropriate hardware, such as a Zigbee or Z-Wave hub, and correct configuration in the Home Assistant user interface. We provided detailed instructions to assist you with this process.

Additionally, we addressed common issues and their solutions in the troubleshooting section. This can help you troubleshoot and optimize your Zigbee and Z-Wave integration in Home Assistant.

With the integration of Zigbee and Z-Wave, you gain numerous opportunities to expand your smart home system. You can seamlessly integrate devices from different brands into your network and make use of extensive automation and control options.

5 Home Assistant Basic Configuration

In this chapter, we'll focus on the basic configuration of Home Assistant. You'll learn how to set up your devices in Home Assistant, create areas for better organization, configure device groups, create a dashboard, set up basic scripts, and troubleshoot common issues. These fundamental steps are essential for making the most of Home Assistant.

After this chapter, your Home Assistant dashboard could look something like this:

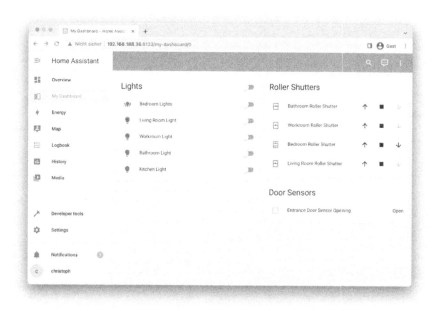

Figure 46 Home Assistant Target Dashboard Configuration

5.1 Setting Up Areas

Setting up areas in Home Assistant allows you to organize your devices and entities based on their locations or functions. By creating areas, you can establish a better structure in your smart home system and simplify device management. In this chapter, we'll show you how to set up areas in Home Assistant.

Step 1: Planning Your Areas

Before you begin setting up areas, it's advisable to do some planning. Think about how you want to organize your devices and entities and what areas you want to create. For example, you could define areas like "Living Room," "Bedroom," "Kitchen," or "Outdoor."

Step 2: Creating Areas

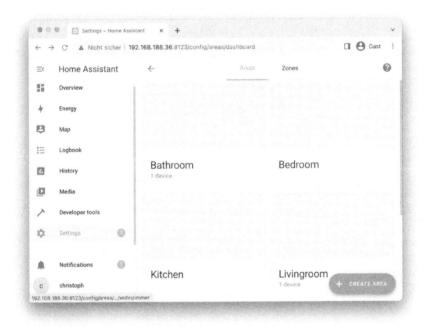

Figure 47 Areas in Home Assistant

Open the Home Assistant user interface and navigate to the Settings. Then, open "Devices & Services" and click on "Areas & Zones." Here, you can create areas based on your planning by clicking the "Create Area" button at the bottom. Give each area a meaningful name that represents its location or function. You can also use icons or images to visually label the areas.

Step 3: Assigning Devices and Entities to Areas

Once you've created the areas, you can assign your devices and entities to the respective areas. How to do this is explained in the next subsection.

Setting up areas in Home Assistant enables effective organization of your devices and entities. By categorizing your devices into areas based on their locations or functions, you create a better structure and simplify the management of your smart home system. Use this feature to make your smart home more organized and user-friendly.

5.2 Device Configuration

In this section, we'll show you how to identify your devices and make their names more readable. We'll also demonstrate how to assign your devices to areas.

Step 1: Identifying Devices

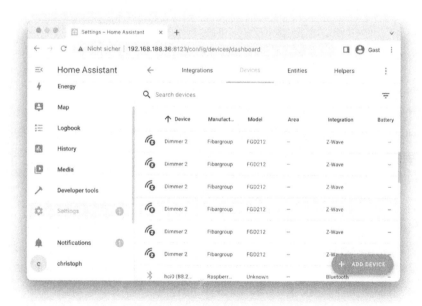

Figure 48 Device Overview

Go to Settings, select "Devices & Services," and navigate to the

"Devices" tab. Here, you'll find a list of the devices you've integrated.

Step 2: Naming Devices and Entities

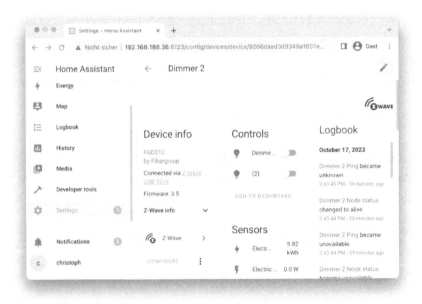

Figure 49 Device View (Fibaro Dimmer)

It's essential to choose clear and easily understandable names for your devices. Avoid cryptic abbreviations or unreadable designations. Instead, use precise and meaningful names that reflect the device type and location. For example, you could use "Living Room Light" for a lamp in the living room.

I recommend giving each device a readable name. To do this, click on the device you want to edit. In the title bar, you'll find the device name. Below that, you'll find all the entities of the device, such as a control for the light. It's also a good idea to give meaningful names to the most important entities of the device.

Step 3: Device Configuration

Click the pencil icon in the top right corner to configure the device. In the popup, you can set a new device name and assign the device to an area.

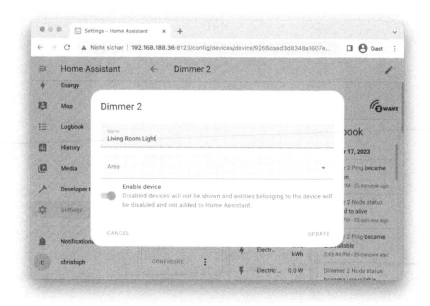

Figure 50 Device Configuration

As mentioned earlier, I also recommend giving readable names to the most important entities. On the device view page, click on the entity you want to edit and, in the popup in the top right corner, click on the gear icon.

Figure 51 Device Entity Popup

Then, assign a readable name to the entity, and equally important, define a readable entity ID following a logical naming scheme (e.g., light.bedroom_ceiling_light, i.e., light.area_position_light).

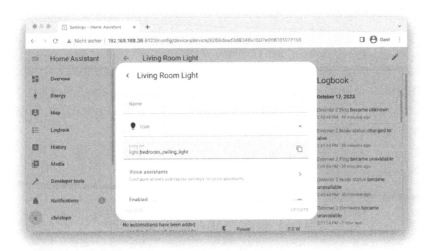

Figure 52 Define Entity ID for Device

By transforming the names of devices and important device entities into a readable format, you can significantly improve the clarity of your configuration. This allows you to easily identify and control your devices, leading to a more pleasant and efficient smart home experience.

5.3 Setting Up Device Groups

Setting up device groups in Home Assistant allows you to group multiple devices together and control them collectively. By creating device groups, you can simplify the operation and automation of your smart home devices.

Step 1: Identify Devices to Group

Before creating a device group, identify the devices you want to group together. Think about which devices share a common function or are used in a specific area of your smart home. For example, you could group all the lights in the living room into a group named "Living Room Lights."

Step 2: Creating the Device Group

Open the Home Assistant user interface and go to Settings. Then, open "Devices & Services" and navigate to "Helpers." Click the "Create Helper" button at the bottom right and choose "Group" in the window that opens. You can also select the group type, such as a light group.

Step 3: Adding Devices to the Group

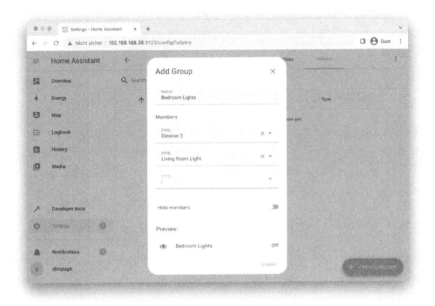

Figure 53 Creating a Device Group

Now, give the device group a name and add the desired devices. Click "Submit" to create the group.

Step 4: Controlling the Device Group

Once you've set up the device group, you can control it as if it were a single device. Use the user interface or automation to turn the group on or off, adjust brightness, or perform other actions. By controlling the device group, all devices within it will be synchronized.

Step 5: Review and Adjust

After creating your device group, review its functionality. Test the group's control and make sure all devices within it are correctly synchronized. If necessary, make adjustments by adding or removing devices or editing the group's configuration.

5.4 Setting Up a Dashboard

A dashboard is a custom interface that allows you to display and manage essential information and controls for your smart home in one central location. In this chapter, we'll show you how to create a dashboard using Lovelace, a popular dashboard configuration interface in Home Assistant. We'll focus on creating a dashboard that enables the control of blinds, lights, displaying temperature and window opening status, and viewing some scripts.

Step 1: Create a New Dashboard or Customize Existing (Optional)

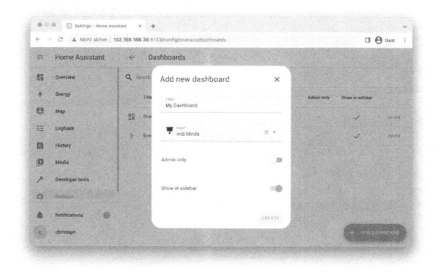

Figure 54 Adding a New Dashboard

Open the Home Assistant user interface and go to Settings. Open "Dashboards" and choose "Add Dashboard" at the bottom right. This option allows you to create a new dashboard. This step is optional; you can also use the default dashboard for the following steps.

Step 2: Navigate to the Lovelace Configuration Interface

Open the dashboard you want to edit by selecting it in the left sidebar. Then, click on the three-dot icon in the upper right and select "Edit Dashboard."

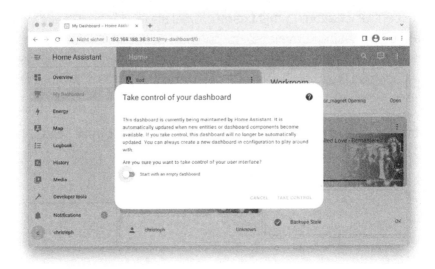

Figure 55 Edit Dashboard

In the following dialog, choose to start with an empty dashboard and click "Take Control."

Step 3: Add Cards and Elements

In the Lovelace configuration interface, you can add cards to display various information and controls. I recommend creating an "Entities" card for your lights, blinds, temperatures, and window or door sensors and then enhance your dashboard with other card types.

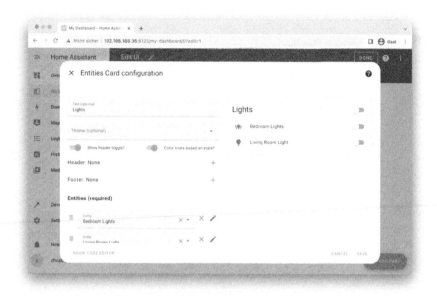

Figure 56 Example Card for Lights

Step 4: Save and View the Dashboard

Once you've made the desired customizations, save the Lovelace configuration and view your dashboard. You should now see your personalized dashboard, enabling you to control blinds, lights, display temperature and window status, and execute scripts.

You can further customize the dashboard by adding additional cards, modifying element grouping, or integrating more functions. Experiment with different layouts and controls to create a dashboard that suits your smart home perfectly.

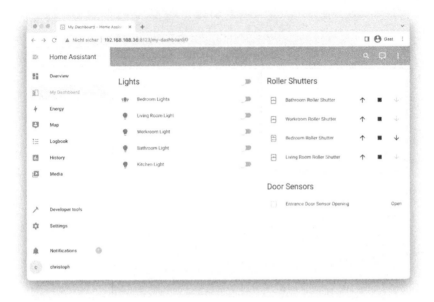

Figure 57 Example Dashboard

By setting up a dashboard, you've created a central hub for controlling your blinds, lights, and viewing critical information. Enjoy the convenience of managing and monitoring your smart home through the Lovelace dashboard.

5.5 Troubleshooting and Common Issues

In this chapter, we address common issues related to the basic configuration of Home Assistant. Here are some common problems you might encounter and possible solutions:

Problem 1: Configuration Errors in Device Setup

- Check if you've installed the required integrations and components to properly support the devices.

Problem 2: Difficulty Setting Up Areas

- Ensure you use correct names and designations for the areas.

- Verify that devices are correctly assigned to their respective areas.

- Check if the areas are displayed correctly in the user interface and that you've configured the desired control options for the areas.

Problem 3: Issues with Device Group Setup

- Ensure that device groups are displayed in the user interface, and the desired control options for the groups are configured.

- Verify that you're using the correct entities and attributes for device groups.

Problem 4: Difficulty Setting Up a Dashboard

- Ensure that the desired views, cards, and elements in the configuration are correctly defined.

- Check if the dashboard is displayed correctly in the user interface, and you've configured the desired controls and functions for the dashboard.

For persistent problems you can't solve on your own, I recommend using Home Assistant's community forums and resources. There, you'll find an active community of users who can assist with troubleshooting and problem-solving.

If you encounter a different issue and can't find a solution despite internet research, feel free to reach out to me at info@rothech.com. I am happy to assist.

5.6 Summary

Chapter 5 has guided us through the basic configuration of Home Assistant, covering essential aspects for a smooth smart home experience. We've delved into configuring devices, explored the setup of areas and device groups, and performed dashboard creation with Lovelace. Additionally, we've discussed troubleshooting and common issues in using Home Assistant.

Configuring devices forms the foundation of our smart homes. By selecting the right platforms and integrations and integrating devices correctly, we can fully utilize their functions. Setting up areas allows us to better organize our homes and enhance device control in specific rooms or zones. Device groups' establishment lets us apply actions to multiple devices simultaneously, improving user-friendliness.

The dashboard is the heart of our smart homes, offering a custom view and control of our devices. We've learned how to create views, cards, and elements to make desired information and functions easily accessible. The example dashboard YAML has shown us how to use the configuration file to customize and expand our dashboard.

We've also discussed key solutions for common problems in Home Assistant.

6 Alexa Voice Configuration

Figure 58 Amazon Echo with Alexa

Integrating voice control into our smart home provides a convenient way to manage our devices and automations. In this chapter, we will focus on configuring Alexa as a voice assistant for Home Assistant. To start, we will provide an overview of the various Alexa integration options. There are several approaches to connect Alexa with Home Assistant, and we will explore the pros and cons, as well as the features of each method. As with any technical setup, problems may arise, so we will also address troubleshooting and common issues that can occur during the configuration of the Alexa integration.

Important: To control your devices with Alexa, you need at least one Amazon Echo device in your household. For example, if you only have Sonos devices with Alexa in your household, you won't be able to control devices using it. Once you have an Amazon Echo in your household, you can access your devices via Alexa, including Sonos devices.

6.1 Overview of Alexa Integration Options

In this section, we will provide a comprehensive overview of the different Alexa integration options. We will familiarize ourselves with the following choices:

1. **Home Assistant Cloud**: Home Assistant Cloud offers seamless integration between Home Assistant and Alexa. By using the paid cloud services, you can easily control your devices and automations with voice commands. This integration offers high reliability and performance as it connects via a secure internet connection.

2. **Emulated Hue Integration**: The Emulated Hue Integration allows Home Assistant to emulate a Philips Hue Bridge, enabling you to control your devices through Alexa by recognizing them as Hue-compatible devices. This open-source solution doesn't require additional paid services and offers flexible configuration.

If you're looking for a straightforward way to integrate Alexa and are willing to pay a few euros per month, we recommend the "Home Assistant Cloud" solution. If you're tech-savvy, want to avoid monthly costs, and can tolerate some occasional quirks (e.g., Alexa error messages), we suggest the "Emulated Hue" approach.

6.2 Alexa Voice Control with Home Assistant Cloud (Paid)

Home Assistant Cloud offers several advantages for Alexa voice control:

1. Reliability

2. Easy Configuration, saving time

It's essential to note that using Home Assistant Cloud comes at a cost. **You'll need to subscribe** to access the cloud services. However, this subscription allows you to have reliable and powerful integration with Alexa.

To set up Home Assistant Cloud for voice control, follow these steps:

1. **Subscribe**: Sign up for a Home Assistant Cloud subscription. Please note that using the cloud services requires a paid fee. Open the Home Assistant settings, navigate to "Home Assistant Cloud," and select the "Start your free 1-month trial" option. Follow the instructions.

Figure 59 Activate Home Assistant Cloud

2. **Enable Alexa & Grant Permissions:** In the settings, go to "Voice Assistants," enable Alexa, and, after activation, navigate to "Make available." Here, you can select the entities you want to control via Alexa.

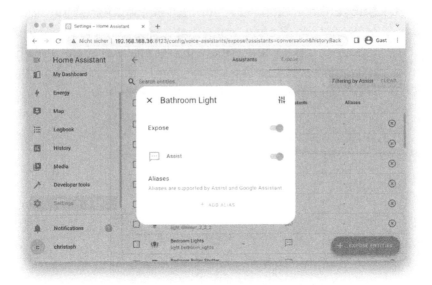

Figure 60 Make an Entity Available via Alexa

3. **Activate the Alexa Skill:** In your Alexa app on your smartphone, visit the Alexa Skills Store and search for the Home Assistant Smart Home Skill. Enable the skill and link it to your Home Assistant Cloud account. Follow the instructions to establish the connection.

4. **Discover Devices:** After activating the skill, you can have Alexa search for Home Assistant devices by saying "Alexa, discover new devices." This will make your devices and entities available in the Alexa app.

5. **Use Voice Commands:** After successful setup, you can now control your Home Assistant devices with Alexa voice commands. Simply say "Alexa," followed by your desired command, e.g., "Turn on the living room light."

It's essential to note that the exact steps may vary depending on the version of Home Assistant you're using and your individual settings. Consult the documentation and guides provided by Home Assistant and Home Assistant Cloud for detailed setup instructions.

6.3 Alexa Voice Control with Emulated Hue Integration (Open Source)

The Emulated Hue Integration allows you to control Home Assistant with Alexa voice commands without relying on the paid Home Assistant Cloud. This open-source integration lets you configure your Home Assistant devices and entities to be recognized and controlled by Alexa.

Here's a guide on setting up the Emulated Hue Integration:

1. **Enable Emulated Hue Integration:** To do this, you need to modify the Home Assistant configuration file.

    1. Navigate to "Settings" > "Add-ons" > "File Editor.". *If you don't have "File Editor" yet, install it via the "Add-on Store".*

    2. Click "Start" and wait for a few seconds, then open the user interface.

    3. Click on the folder icon in the upper right and navigate to "config/configuration.yaml."

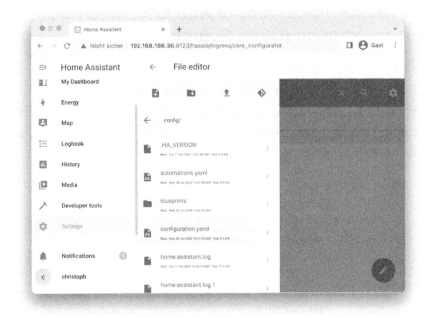

Figure 61 File Editor - configuration.yaml

4. Enable the Emulated Hue Integration by adding the following configuration at the end of the file:

```
emulated_hue:
  listen_port: 80
```

Code 1 Emulated Hue Configuration in configuration.yaml

2. **Configure Devices:** By default, all your devices will be made available through the Emulated Hue Integration for Alexa. However, we recommend only providing the devices and entities you want to control via Alexa to avoid potential issues like slow response times. You can adjust your configuration as follows:

```
emulated_hue:
  listen_port: 80
  expose_by_default: false
  entities:
    light.alle_lampen:
```

```
    hidden: false
light.bedroom_ceiling_light:
    hidden: false
light.bedroom_lightstrip:
    hidden: false
```

Code 2 Emulated Hue Configuration with Entities

List all the entity IDs you want to make available to Alexa under "entities."

3. **Save Your Emulated Hue Configuration**: Click the red save icon in the upper right to save the new configuration.

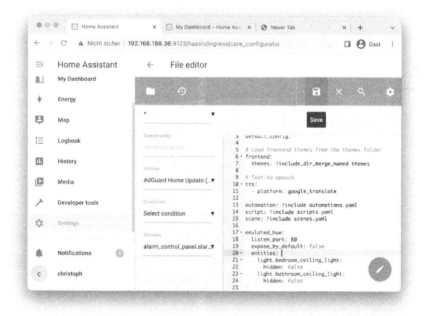

Figure 62 Save Emulated Hue Configuration

4. **Test Your Emulated Hue Configuration:** Restart your Home Assistant from the File Editor to activate Emulated Hue and make your devices available. Click on the gear icon in the upper right and select "Restart Home Assistant."

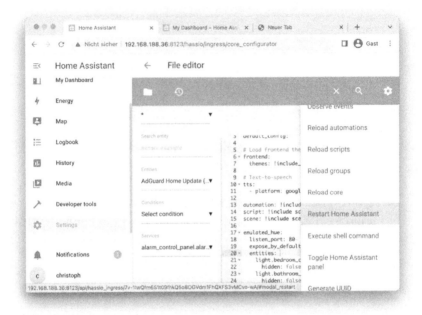

Figure 63 Restart Home Assistant

5. **Discover Alexa Devices:** Open the Alexa app on your mobile device, go to settings, select "Add a device," and then "Set up a new device." Alexa will search for available devices and should recognize the emulated Hue Bridge.

6. **Use Voice Commands:** After successful setup, you can now control your Home Assistant devices with Alexa voice commands. Simply say "Alexa," followed by your desired command, e.g., "Turn on the living room light."

It's important to be aware that the Emulated Hue Integration may have some limitations. Not all device types and functions may be fully supported. Check Home Assistant's documentation and guides for detailed information on configuration and compatibility.

6.4 Troubleshooting and Common Issues

In this chapter, we address common problems related to integrating

Alexa into Home Assistant and present solutions to these challenges. If you encounter issues or Alexa doesn't work as expected with Home Assistant, you'll find helpful tips and tricks here to resolve them.

Problem 1: Alexa Doesn't Recognize My Devices.

- Ensure you have at least one original Amazon Echo device in your smart home.

- Verify that the Emulated Hue Integration is correctly installed and active.

- Make sure the selected devices are configured in the Emulated Hue Integration, and your entities are correctly included.

- Check if Alexa has completed device discovery, and the emulated Hue Bridge is recognized in the Alexa app.

Problem 2: Alexa Can't Control My Devices.

- Confirm that your voice commands are correctly formulated and that device names are pronounced accurately in Alexa.

- Check if the desired actions and control commands in Home Assistant are configured correctly.

- Investigate possible conflicts with other integration or automation rules that may affect device control.

Problem 3: Delays in Alexa Response Time.

- Check the network connection and stability of your Home Assistant system.

- Ensure that both Home Assistant and the Emulated Hue Integration are up to date, and all necessary updates are installed.

- If needed, reduce the number of active devices and automations in Home Assistant to optimize performance.

Problem 4: Alexa Generates Error Messages or Unexpected Responses.

- Review the logs and error messages in Home Assistant to identify potential configuration errors or inconsistencies.

- Update the firmware or software of both Home Assistant and the devices you want to control with Alexa.

- Verify that voice commands and associated automations or scenes in Home Assistant are correctly set up.

Problem 5: Alexa Doesn't Respond to My Voice Commands.

- Ensure that your Home Assistant system is properly connected to the internet.

- Investigate potential issues with the Alexa app or Alexa devices by testing other functions or services.

- Check the connection between Home Assistant and the Emulated Hue Integration to ensure it is active and functional.

For persistent issues that you cannot resolve on your own, I recommend using the community forums and resources provided by Home Assistant. There, you'll find an active community of users who can assist with troubleshooting and problem-solving.

If you encounter a different issue and can't find a solution despite internet research, feel free to reach out to me at info@rothech.com. I am happy to assist.

6.5 Summary

In this chapter, we explored the integration of Home Assistant and

Alexa for voice control. We learned about various Alexa integration options, including the use of the paid Home Assistant Cloud and the Emulated Hue Integration as an open-source solution.

With Home Assistant Cloud, we can control Home Assistant through voice commands with Alexa by synchronizing our devices and automations. It offers user-friendly setup and allows us to seamlessly connect our smart home devices with Alexa.

Alternatively, we can use the Emulated Hue Integration to link Home Assistant with Alexa. This requires some manual configuration steps but provides a free and open solution for voice control.

We also took a look at potential problems and their solutions that may arise during Alexa integration. It's crucial to be vigilant about connectivity issues, authentication errors, and other difficulties to ensure smooth voice control.

With the various integration options and the troubleshooting tips provided, you can successfully connect Home Assistant to Alexa and control your smart home devices via voice commands. Voice control offers a convenient way to operate your devices and automations, further enhancing the comfort of your smart home.

7 Voice Output with Sonos

Figure 64 Sonos One Speaker

Integrating Sonos into Home Assistant allows us to expand our smart home systems with voice output capabilities. In this chapter, we will explore the reasons why Sonos is a popular choice for voice output and learn how to set up Sonos in Home Assistant.

7.1 Why Sonos?

Sonos is a popular choice for voice output in Home Assistant for several reasons. Here are some of the key advantages and features that make Sonos the preferred voice output device:

1. **Seamless Integration with Home Assistant**: Setting up Sonos in Home Assistant is straightforward and allows for smooth integration. This enables users to control voice outputs conveniently through the Home Assistant user interface or automations.

2. **Versatile Control Options**: Sonos offers flexible control of voice output. With integration into Home Assistant, mobile apps, voice assistants like Alexa or Google Assistant, and physical controls, users have various options to control the

playback of voice messages.

3. **Multiroom Audio**: Sonos supports multiroom audio, allowing multiple Sonos speakers throughout the house to be synchronized. This enables voice output throughout the entire home by playing messages on multiple speakers simultaneously.

4. **Expandability**: Sonos offers a wide range of products, including various speaker models and subwoofers. These can be combined and expanded as needed to create a custom audio system.

With these features, Sonos is a powerful solution for voice output in Home Assistant. Excellent sound quality, versatile control options, and seamless integration make Sonos a popular choice for those who want to deliver voice messages and notifications in their smart home with precision and quality.

7.2 Setting up Sonos and TTS in Home Assistant

Setting up Sonos and Text-to-Speech (TTS) in Home Assistant allows for the seamless integration and control of Sonos speakers for voice output and media playback. Here is a step-by-step guide on how to set up Sonos in Home Assistant:

1. **Install the Sonos Integration:**
   - Open the Home Assistant user interface and go to the "Settings" menu.
   - Select "Integrations" and search for the Sonos integration.
   - Click "Add" and follow the instructions to install the integration.
2. **Configure the Sonos Speakers:**
   - Please follow Chapter 5.2 to give meaningful names to the speakers and their entities in Home Assistant.

- The "media_player" entities are the most important ones, as they allow you to address the Sonos speakers.

3. **Set up Google TTS in configuration.yaml:**
   - Open the Home Assistant user interface and go to the "Settings" menu.
   - Select "Add-ons" and then open "File editor." If the File editor is not running, click "Start" and wait a few seconds. Then, click "Open the user interface."
   - Open the file "config/configuration.yaml" by clicking on the folder icon in the upper right.
   - Add the following code at the end of the file:

```
tts:
  - platform: google_translate
    service_name: google_translate_say
```

Code 3 Google TTS Configuration in configuration.yaml

- Click the red save icon and then restart Home Assistant by clicking on the gear icon and selecting "Restart Home Assistant."

With the setup of Sonos and TTS in Home Assistant, you have created the foundation to use Sonos speakers for voice output and media file playback. You can now play notifications, voice messages, or even music through the Sonos speakers in your smart home and seamlessly integrate them into your automations and scenes.

7.3 Voice Output with Sonos

Voice output with Sonos in Home Assistant allows you to play custom voice messages through your configured Sonos speakers. Here is a guide on how to do this using a script:

1. **Create a Script:**

- Open the Home Assistant user interface and go to "Settings."
- Then, select "Automations & Scripts" and click "Scripts" at the top.
- Click "Create a new script" at the bottom right of the pop-up dialog, and once again, on "Create a new script."
- Click the three-dot icon in the upper right and select "Edit as YAML."

2. **Define the Action:**

Within the script, you need to define the action that triggers the voice output. Use the service action "tts.google_translate_say" and input the required parameters:

- **entity_id**: Specify the entity of the Sonos speaker where the voice output should be played.
- **message**: Enter the text or voice message you want to play.

Example:

```
alias: New Script
sequence:
  - service: tts.google_translate_say
    data:
      entity_id: media_player.wohnzimmer
      message: "May the force be with you."
```

Code 4 TTS Output Script Example

3. **Save the Script:** Click "Save" to save the script and make it available.
4. **Test the Script:** To test the script, you can either manually execute it or integrate it into an automation. When the script is executed, the Sonos speaker should play the defined voice message.

Note: Ensure that the Sonos speaker is turned on and connected to the network for successful voice output.

With this script, you can now play custom voice messages through your configured Sonos speakers. You can use the script in automations to deliver welcome messages, notifications, or reminders through Sonos, making your smart home even more interactive.

7.4 Troubleshooting and Common Issues

Voice output with Sonos in Home Assistant may encounter occasional problems. Here are some common issues and potential solutions:

Problem 1: Sonos Speaker Not Detected

- Check if the Sonos speaker is correctly configured in Home Assistant.

- Ensure that the Sonos speaker is powered on and connected to the same network as Home Assistant.

- Restart both the Sonos speaker and Home Assistant.

Problem 2: Voice Output Not Playing

- Verify that the script is correctly created and configured.

- Ensure that the Sonos speaker entity is correctly specified in the script's action.

- Check the volume of the Sonos speaker and ensure it is not muted.

Problem 3: Delay in Voice Output

- Ensure your network is stable and not experiencing connectivity issues.

- Check the performance of your Home Assistant host and optimize resource allocation if necessary.

- Update the firmware of your Sonos speaker to address potential issues.

Problem 4: Sonos Speaker Controlled by Other Devices

- Check if other devices or applications accessing the Sonos speaker are affecting control.

- Disconnect other applications or disable their access to the Sonos speaker to avoid conflicts.

If you encounter issues that you cannot resolve on your own, you can utilize the Home Assistant community forums and resources. There, you will find an active user community that can assist with troubleshooting and problem-solving.

If you encounter a different issue and can't find a solution despite internet research, feel free to reach out to me at info@rothech.com. I am happy to assist.

7.5 Summary

In this chapter, we explored voice output with Sonos in Home Assistant. Sonos provides a powerful way to deliver voice commands and notifications in your smart home.

First, we discussed the benefits of Sonos as a voice output option in Home Assistant. High sound quality, support for multiple speakers, and seamless integration make Sonos a popular choice.

Next, we covered the setup of Sonos in Home Assistant. You learned how to connect your Sonos speakers to Home Assistant and configure them correctly, enabling seamless use of your Sonos speakers within Home Assistant.

We also detailed how to set up voice output using a script. You learned how to create the script, define the desired voice message, and select the Sonos speaker entity for playback. This allows you to conveniently play voice commands or notifications through your Sonos speakers.

Furthermore, we addressed troubleshooting and common problems. If you encounter issues such as Sonos speakers not being detected or delays in voice output, you received potential solutions to address these problems.

In conclusion, voice output with Sonos in Home Assistant is an advanced feature that may require some patience and configuration adjustments. With the right setup and community support, you can fully utilize the benefits of voice control and voice output in your smart home.

8 Push Notifications with iOS and Android

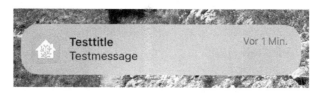

Figure 65 Home Assistant Push Notification

In the following chapter, we will explore the setup of push notifications for iOS and Android in Home Assistant. Push notifications are a convenient way to stay informed about important events and updates in your smart home, even when you don't actively open the Home Assistant Companion App.

First, we will provide an overview of the various options for push notifications. Then, we will focus on setting up push notifications using the Home Assistant Companion App.

8.1 Overview of Push Notification Options

There are several options available to configure push notifications in Home Assistant. We will take a closer look at the following main options:

1. **Home Assistant Cloud (Paid):** Home Assistant Cloud offers an integrated push notification feature. With this option, you can send notifications directly to iOS and Android devices without the need for additional configuration or integrations.

2. **Home Assistant Companion App:** The official Home Assistant Companion App for iOS and Android allows you to set up personalized push notifications. You can create individual notifications for specific events or automations and customize the settings to your preferences.

3. **Third-Party Integrations:** There are also third-party integrations that allow you to receive push notifications from Home Assistant on your mobile device. Popular options include integrations with Telegram, Pushbullet, Notify, and more. However, these integrations often require additional configuration steps.

In the following chapter, we will delve into setting up push notifications using the Home Assistant Companion App. This option provides a simple and free way to establish push notifications.

8.2 Setting up Push Notifications with the Home Assistant Companion App

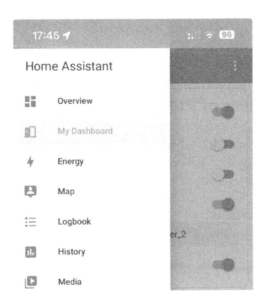

Figure 66 Home Assistant Companion App

The Home Assistant Companion App allows you to receive push notifications on your iOS or Android device. Here is a structured guide on setting up push notifications using the Home Assistant Companion App:

Step 1: Install the Home Assistant Companion App

- Go to the App Store or Google Play Store on your iOS or Android device.

- Search for "Home Assistant Companion" and install the app.

Step 2: Connect the App to Your Home Assistant Server

- Open the Home Assistant Companion App on your device.

- Tap on the button to add a new server.

- Enter the URL of your Home Assistant server and authenticate if required.

- Wait for the app to establish a connection to the server.

Step 3: Enable Push Notifications in the Settings

- Go to the settings of the Home Assistant Companion App.

- Look for notification settings.

- Enable push notifications and allow the app to display notifications on your device.

Step 4: Test the Push Notifications

- Navigate in the Home Assistant user interface to "Developer Tools" and then to "Services."

- Use the text field under "Service" to search for "notify" and select the device to which you want to send a message, e.g., "notify.mobile_app_iphone_c."

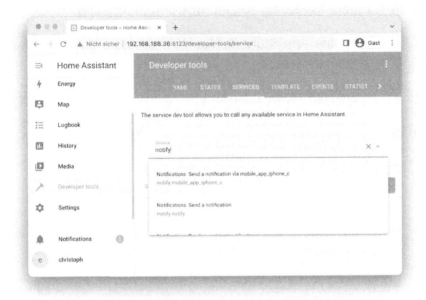

Figure 67 Developer Tools - Services - Push Notification

- Enter a test message (under "Message") and a test title (under "Title"), and then click "Call Service."

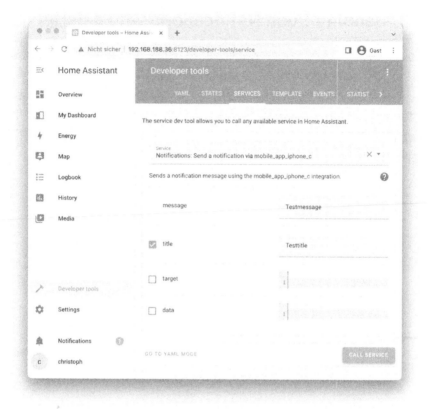

Figure 68 Send Test Message

- You should receive the push notification on your smartphone.

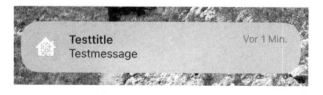

Figure 69 Example Notification

With these steps, you have successfully set up push notifications using the Home Assistant Companion App. You can now receive personalized notifications from your Home Assistant server on your iOS or Android device.

8.3 Sending Push Notifications with a Script

To ensure that your push notifications work correctly, you can use a sample script to trigger a test notification. If you have already successfully sent a push notification in Chapter 8.2 through the user interface, you can simply view the YAML script code that sent the notification. Just click on "YAML mode" in the lower left to view the relevant code:

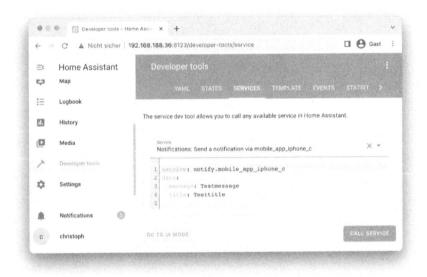

Figure 70 Push Notification YAML Code

Here is a simple example script that sends a push notification:

```
alias: Push-Notification-Test
sequence:
  - service: notify.mobile_app_dein_gerät
    data:
      message: "Testmessage"
      title: "Testtitle"
```

Code 5 Push Notification Script Example

In this script, the service **notify.mobile_app_your_device** is called to send a notification to your device. Make sure to replace your_device with the actual name of your device as displayed in the Home Assistant Companion App.

To use the script, follow these steps:

1. Open the Home Assistant user interface in your web browser.

2. Navigate to the automations page or the scripts page in Home Assistant.

3. Create a new script and paste the example code shown above.

4. Save the script.

After saving the script, you can execute it to test the push notification. If everything is configured correctly, you should receive a notification on your iOS or Android device.

By running this example script, you can ensure that your push notifications are working, and you can use it as a starting point to create custom notifications with specific content and actions.

8.4 Troubleshooting and Common Issues

While setting up push notifications with the Home Assistant Companion App typically goes smoothly, occasional problems may arise. Here are some common issues and possible solutions:

Problem 1: Push Notifications Not Received

- First, check your device's network connection and ensure it is connected to the internet.

- Make sure you have the latest version of the Home Assistant Companion App installed on your device.

- Verify the configuration of push notifications in Home Assistant to ensure everything is set up correctly.

- Retest the notification to ensure it's not a temporary issue.

Problem 2: Delayed Delivery of Push Notifications

- Check your device's settings to ensure it's not in power-saving or "Do Not Disturb" mode, as this can affect notification delivery.

- Verify your device's network connection and ensure it has a stable internet connection.

- Ensure that the Home Assistant Companion App is running in the background and has not been closed by a task manager app or similar.

Problem 3: Notifications Contain Incorrect or Incomplete Information

- Review the configuration of your notifications in Home Assistant and ensure the correct data and variables are being used.

- Check for errors or inconsistencies in the script or automation that triggers the notification.

Problem 4: Notifications Not Displayed on a Specific Device

- Ensure that the device in question is correctly connected to the Home Assistant Companion App.

- Check the push notification settings on the device to ensure they are not blocked or disabled.

Problem 5: Other Technical Issues or Irregularities

- Restart the device in question and reopen the Home Assistant Companion App.

- Check the logs in Home Assistant to identify any errors or hints of problems.

If you continue to experience issues with push notifications, and the solutions mentioned above do not help, I recommend reaching out to the Home Assistant community or support.

If you encounter a different issue and can't find a solution despite internet research, feel free to reach out to me at info@rothech.com. I am happy to assist.

8.5 Summary

In this chapter, we explored the setup of push notifications for iOS and Android in Home Assistant. We provided an overview of the various options for push notifications and specifically focused on setting them up using the Home Assistant Companion App.

We explained step by step how to install and configure the Home Assistant Companion App to receive push notifications. Additionally, we showed how you can use notifications in automations and scripts to send important information to your mobile device.

Furthermore, we discussed common issues and their potential solutions. From notifications not being delivered to incorrect information in notifications, we provided tips on how to address these problems.

Push notifications are an effective way to stay informed about important events and states in your Home Assistant system. With the right settings and the ability to overcome potential issues, you can make full use of push notifications and enhance your smart home experience.

9 Outlook

Congratulations! You have now built a solid foundation and acquired numerous skills to manage and automate your smart home with Home Assistant. With the knowledge you've gained, you are ready to take your smart home to the next level and implement further exciting smart home automations.

Now is the perfect time to unleash your creativity and explore additional use cases for your smart home. You can integrate new devices and sensors, create custom automations, and make your home even more efficient and comfortable. Experiment with different trigger events, conditions, and actions to develop tailored automations that precisely meet your needs.

Utilize the Home Assistant community to connect with other smart home enthusiasts, gather new ideas, and receive support for your projects. The community offers a wealth of knowledge, experiences, and solutions that can help you achieve any automation goal.

Expand your smart home according to your vision and continually optimize it to create a living experience perfectly tailored to you. From lighting control and energy efficiency to security and comfort, there are countless opportunities to further enhance your smart home.

Enjoy the freedom and flexibility that Home Assistant provides to design your smart home according to your individual preferences. Dive into new projects, try out new integrations, and let your creativity run wild. With Home Assistant, you have the tool to create a truly intelligent and personalized smart home.

Now it's up to you to continue your smart home journey and implement additional smart home automations and optimizations. Use the knowledge you've acquired, experiment, and enjoy the benefits of a smart and automated home. The possibilities are endless, and with Home Assistant, you are well-equipped to achieve any automation goal.

Embark on your journey and discover how far you can optimize and automate your smart home. Good luck, and continue to enjoy your intelligent home!

On a personal note:

Your opinion matters to me! If you have suggestions for improvement or ideas to expand the content, I would appreciate your feedback. Feel free to send me an email at info@rothech.com. Your input helps make the book even more useful and engaging.

If you enjoy the book, I would be grateful for an Amazon review. Your review is crucial for other readers and contributes to the creation of future works on this topic.

Thank you for your support! 😊